the great PYRAMID

Author: Anne Millard
Consultant: Helen Strudwick

ticktock
MEDIA

Copyright © *ticktock* Entertainment Ltd 2005

First published in Great Britain in 2005 by *ticktock* Media Ltd.,

Unit 2, Orchard Business Centre, North Farm Road, Tunbridge Wells, Kent, TN2 3XF

We would like to thank: Alison Howard, Susan Barraclough, Elizabeth Wiggans and Jenni Rainsford for their help with this book.

ISBN 1 86007 595 9 PB

Printed in China

A CIP catalogue record for this book is available from the British Library.

Contents

Introduction

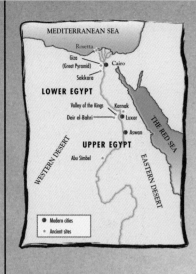

The Great Pyramid certainly lives up to its name – it is huge! It was originally 147 metres tall and at its base the sides measured just over 230 metres. It is estimated that over two million blocks of stone were used to build it. Even today, when people are used to large buildings, they still gaze in wonder at the Great Pyramid's majestic bulk. It is easy to wonder why the ancient Egyptians spent so much time, energy and resources on building such a colossal monument.

WHY WAS IT BUILT?

The Great Pyramid is the tomb of the King of Upper and Lower Egypt – Khufu – who lived about 2,600 BC. The Great Pyramid had several different purposes and a number of different symbolic meanings, as did most things in ancient Egyptian religious beliefs. The ancient Egyptians believed that when they died, they were reborn into the Next World – which was like the Egypt they loved, but made perfect. To enjoy life properly in the Next World, the Egyptians believed that a person's spirit needed to return to its body occasionally. That was why they invented the process we call 'mummification' – a way to preserve the body after death.

AN ELABORATE TOMB

The Egyptians also believed that they could take all the things they needed to live comfortably in the Next World by placing the objects in their tombs. The Great Pyramid was the king's tomb, specially designed to give maximum protection to his body and his treasure. It also provided a place where priests could make offerings to his spirit for ever. The pyramid and any treasure in it also had a symbolic significance – displaying the power and glory of the king to his people, future generations and the gods. The Egyptians believed that their king was more than just a man. They considered him to be an earthly form of the god Horus (who had once ruled Egypt himself). This made the king a sacred, part-divine being who would become a god himself

The pyramids and Sphinx are silhouetted against the ever-changing colours of the evening sky as Re sinks in glory into the West and enters the Underworld. He will be reborn in the East in the morning.

after death. In heaven, the king was thought to go on caring for his subjects, just as he had done on Earth. The pyramid was also regarded as the earthly gateway through which the king's spirit would pass before joining the gods in the Next World.

GATEWAY TO THE NEXT WORLD

In the beginning, the priests taught that there was nothing but water. Then the god Atum, who dwelt in this ocean, thrust up the first land. The sun god Re stood on this mound of land and created the whole world and everything in it. The mound was Re's most holy symbol and the Egyptians saw it as a symbol not only of creation and birth, but also of rebirth into the Next World. What better place to bury a king than under a representation of the sun god's most holy symbol?

The only portrait of Khufu found so far is this tiny statuette, just 7.6 cm tall.

The interior walls of this pyramid, belonging to one of Khufu's descendents, are covered with the spells, prayers and hymns from the Pyramid Texts.

The word 'pyramid' comes from an ancient Greek word. The Egyptian equivalent was originally 'mr', meaning 'a place of ascension'. An Egyptian text, known as the Pyramid Texts, states: 'I have trodden on the sun's rays, using them as a ramp to go up ...'. So, although the pyramid did not reach all the way to heaven, it symbolised a ramp made of sunbeams that would carry the king to join the god Re in the sky.

CHAPTER 1

How it was built

No evidence exists that verifies the exact building methods used by the ancient Egyptians, but many highly plausible theories have been considered over the years. We know that, whatever the method, a pyramid would have taken a long time to build. Therefore, when Khufu came to the throne, one of his very first acts would have been to order the building of his pyramid. The Egyptians did not have cranes or mechanical diggers, but they did have great ingenuity.

This 19th century ad illustration shows a village at the foot of the Giza Plateau. The waters of the Nile's annual flooding still crept up to the foot of the Plateau until the building of modern dams at Aswan.

One of the first people to write about their visit to Egypt was a Greek called Herodotus who visited Egypt in about 450 BC. His book reports that Khufu was a cruel tyrant who oppressed his people and reduced the country to poverty in order to build his pyramid. An earlier papyrus from about 1,900 BC gives a similar impression of Khufu. It is also possible that Herodotus had a deep distrust of eastern kings, because of the suffering inflicted on the Greeks by the Persians.

LOCATION

The choice of site for Khufu's pyramid was important. Sakkara, the nearest site to the capital, already had Zoser's Step Pyramid and Khufu's father, Sneferu, had built to the south at Dahshur. Khufu preferred the Giza Plateau

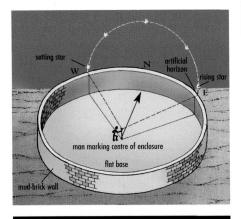

The Egyptians believed a pyramid's sides needed to precisely face north, south, east and west – so calculations would have been taken very carefully.

for his pyramid. This site had several advantages. The rocky plateau rose sharply above the river valley, so was very imposing. It was nearly flat, it was good, solid stone to build on and there was plenty of local limestone, which could be used for the building of the pyramid. It was

also only a few miles north of Memphis, the capital.

PLANNING

The first job would probably have been to draw up a plan for the king's approval. Presumably, the next challenge would have been to fix exactly where north lay. Many historians believe this would have been necessary because the pyramid had to have each side perfectly oriented with one of the points of the compass – north, south, east and west – for the rituals to work properly. To find north, the surveyors would probably have first built a round, high-walled enclosure out of mud-brick (*see diagram, above left*). A priest-surveyor then probably stood at the centre of the circle. When a particular star first appeared in the sky (*rising star*), just above the eastern wall (*artificial horizon*), his assistant would have marked the spot in the ground. The pair would then have had to wait to mark the point where the star set in the west

(*setting star*). These two points and the place where the priest had stood then formed a triangle – the angle of which would have been divided to give them the measurement for north. The pyramid's sides would have then been marked out on the ground. The area would then have been

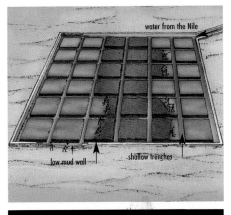

Next, the site would be divided into squares. Water-filled channels would be used as a measure for clearing a smooth surface.

divided into sections with channels cut between them and filled with water (*see diagram, above*). Then, workmen would have cut away all the rock until it was level with the surface of the water. Then, the water would have been drained out and the small channels filled in. They would

The Great Pyramid

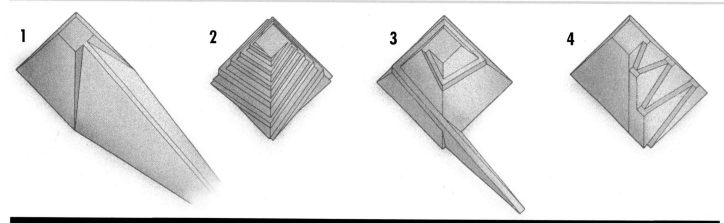

There are several theories about how ramps were constructed. Four are illustrated here: (1) a straight, sloping ramp up one face; (2) several ramps starting at the base and wrapping around the pyramid; (3) a single ramp wrapping around the pyramid; (4) a zigzag-ramp on one side of the pyramid.

now have a flat surface, exactly orientated for building to start.

MOUNTAINS OF STONE

The moment Khufu decided to build his pyramid at Giza the order would have gone out to start cutting stones. The limestone for the body of the pyramid would have been quarried at Giza itself, but the fine, white limestone for the casing blocks came from Turah, a quarry on the other side of the Nile. The great slabs of granite for the burial chamber came from Aswan, some 965 kilometres to the south. Other stones such as gleaming alabaster and black basalt came from other quarries in Egypt's deserts. By the time the site was levelled and the main workforce arrived, hundreds of blocks would have been ready and waiting.

HEAVY WORK

Of the 2,300,000 stone blocks in the Great Pyramid, the average weight of each is 2.5 tons, but others are monsters

The construction of the pyramid is now underway. The huge blocks are hauled up the ramp and levered into place.

Tale & customs – GETTING THE FACTS STRAIGHT

The myth that Hebrew slaves built the Great Pyramid during their period in Egypt was started by the great Jewish writer Flavius Josephus (c. AD 37–100). He wrote several books to explain Jewish religion and history to non-Jewish readers. In fact, the pyramids were built more than a thousand years before the period when people from that area of the Near East settled in Egypt. Although much is shrouded in mystery, there is a wealth of archaeological evidence that supports what is commonly accepted to be the pyramid's actual origins.

weighing 15 tons and more. To get a block of stone into place, it would have been levered on to a sledge and secured with ropes. A gang of 10 or more men (according to the size of the block) would then grasp the ropes and haul it along. Another gang of men would walk in front of the stone-hauling team, laying rollers so the sledge would glide along more easily. They poured milk down, which is greasy and would have helped the sledge glide over the rollers. Water may have been splashed on to the rollers because the friction of the sledge on the rollers could otherwise cause them to smoulder.

PAINSTAKING CONSTRUCTION

The first blocks were laid in the centre of the pyramid's base, then the rest of the first layer of stones were placed around them. Finally, the casing stones were positioned on the outside. A ramp of mud bricks, sand and rubble would then have been built so that the next layer of stones could be pulled into place. The ramp was then extended, layer upon layer, until the required height was reached. Finally, a pyramid-shaped capstone would have been placed on top. Some scholars suggest that the capstone was covered with gold, which would dazzle people in the hot Egyptian

Although the casing blocks have been taken from most of the pyramids, the patches that remain show how tightly they fitted, one to the other.

sun. The ramps were then removed from top to bottom, and the casing stones cut to the correct angle. Experts disagree as to how many ramps were used and how they were placed. Some think just one, very long ramp was used. Others believe ramps were built around the four sides of the pyramid as it rose. Whatever method was used, it was a huge job shifting all those blocks. One estimate says workmen would have needed to get one block in place every two minutes. Even when the main pyramid was finished, work was still far from over. A pyramid was simply one part of a whole complex of connected buildings – all of which were vitally important for running the funeral cult after the burial.

CHAPTER 2

History of the pyramids

The ideas and expertise required for building the Great Pyramid can be linked back to the beginning of Egyptian civilisation. The ancient Egyptians did not need help from visitors from other planets or survivors of an older, 'lost', civilisation as some people have suggested. We can trace their efforts at making tombs from simple beginnings, through successes and failures, right up to the Great Pyramid.

WHAT WENT BEFORE?

The first 'ancient Egyptian' graves – dated to c.5,000 BC – were just oval scoops in the sand. The body was wrapped in linen or a mat and surrounded with provisions for the Next World. A mound of sand and stones was raised over the top. The poor went on being buried like that throughout Egyptian history, but as Egypt grew rich, its leaders – chiefs and then kings – wanted bigger, more impressive monuments.

EARLY MASTABAS

These graves were cut deeper, in a neater rectangular shape. The sides were lined with wood or mud bricks and the body was placed in a reed or wooden coffin. The mound over the top was better made too and was eventually replaced by a rectangular mud brick building, the sides of which sloped in slightly. This style of tomb

A very ancient Egyptian. He was buried with his supplies of food and drink and his prized possessions in a shallow grave. The hot desert sand dried out his body and preserved it for some 5,000 years.

Time line

c.5,000–3,100 BC

The Predynastic Period. Egypt is a land of small states that come together into two kingdoms – Upper and Lower Egypt. At first, burials are in scoops in the sand, then they evolve into mud-brick mastabas.

c.3,100–2,686 BC

The Archaic Period. Narmer, King of Upper Egypt, conquers the North and Egypt is united. Dynasties I & II. Kings are buried in large mud-brick mastabas. Memphis is the capital.

The pyramid at Meidum had a stepped core, but with straight sides on the outside. The outer casing collapsed and the inner stepped structure is now visible.

was called a 'mastaba'. The royal mastabas had stone-lined burial chambers surrounded by many rooms, all full with food, tools and weapons, furniture, clothes and jewellery.

THE FIRST PYRAMIDS

About 2,670 BC, an architect called Imhotep built a square, stone mastaba for his king, Zoser. Then he enlarged the mastaba and added other, smaller mastabas on top, thus forming the first 'step' pyramid. Within 70 years these ancient Egyptians made another attempt to improve the design of the kings' funeral monuments. The steps of the last step pyramid (thought to belong to Huni, the last king of Dynasty II) were filled in with sloping blocks. This proved to be disastrous because the outer casing fell away, dragging much of the inside of the pyramid with it. The early kings believed that their spirits would join the Pole Star and the stars that cluster around it above the North Pole. They called them 'the imperishable stars', because they never sank below the horizon, making them a perfect symbol of eternity.

As the sun god Re grew in importance, pyramid design was changed again so it

c. 2,682–2,181 BC

The Old Kingdom. Dynasties III–VI. A time of great achievement. The Step Pyramid is built. From Dynasty IV onwards, pyramids have straight sides. This is when the Giza pyramids were built.

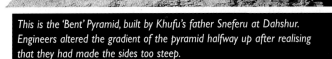

This is the 'Bent' Pyramid, built by Khufu's father Sneferu at Dahshur. Engineers altered the gradient of the pyramid halfway up after realising that they had made the sides too steep.

would aid the passage to Re's side in the afterlife. The next attempt should have been a perfectly shaped pyramid, but again disaster struck. Half-way through building, the architects decided the angle was too steep. They changed it to a gentler slope, which left them with a bent structure. Undaunted, they made another attempt and this time the pyramid was a success. This pyramid is generally believed to be the final resting place of Sneferu, Khufu's father.

THE PHARAOHS

When Khufu died, his son Radjedef came to the throne. The new king immediately started to build his own pyramid at Abu Roash, north of Giza. Radjedef had only a brief reign and his pyramid was never finished. He was succeeded by his younger brother, Khafre, who built the second great pyramid at Giza. It was not quite as tall as his father's, but it was on slightly higher ground, so it looks taller, especially now as some of its casing blocks remain at the top,

Time and weather have not been kind to the Sphinx. Windblown sand constantly erodes its body and vandals have knocked off its nose.

c. 2,181–2,025 BC

The First Intermediate Period. Dynasties VII–X. Egypt descends into chaos with rival kings, civil wars, powerful war-lords and famines.

c. 2,025–1,700 BC

The Middle Kingdom. Dynasties XI–XIII. Egypt is reunited by a Prince of Thebes. Thebes becomes the capital and royal tombs are under great temples. Dynasty XII kings move back north to a site near Memphis and are buried in pyramids. Another period of great cultural achievement.

whereas all Khufu's have since been removed. A great deal of stone had been quarried at Giza, leaving a large rocky outcrop close to where Khafre's Valley Temple was being built. Someone, whose identity is not known,

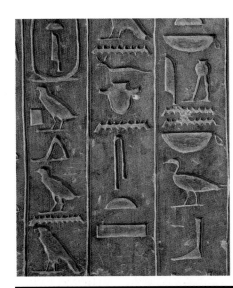

Beautifully carved hieroglyphs in the chambers of later pyramids give us vital clues about religious beliefs in the time of Khufu and for hundreds of years before him.

suggested carving this stone into a sphinx – a lion with a human head. The face may be a portrait of King Khafre.

The sphinx was a form of the sun god who guarded the site. A temple dedicated to him was built in front of his paws. Khafre's son, Menkawre, also built at Giza, but his pyramid was somewhat smaller. The three pyramids follow the line of the solid rock of the plateau, so each one is set slightly back from the other and each has its own clear view of the North, to establish the exact position the priests required.

KHUFU'S HEIRS

Only one other major royal monument was erected at Giza – that of Queen Khentkawes. A rocky outcrop was carved into a square platform and then a mastaba-like tomb was built on top. Queen Khentkawes may even have reigned in her own right for a while. Her sons were the first two kings of Dynasty V.

The kings of Dynasties V and VI went on building pyramids, but none is anywhere near as big as those at Giza, nor were they as well-built. The blocks inside were small, in some cases little more than rubble, and over the years some have collapsed. However, a dramatic development occurred in the chamber of the pyramid of King Unas, last King of Dynasty V, and the walls were covered in

inscriptions. These are known as the *Pyramid Texts* – spells, prayers and rituals. Some of them were very old indeed, a few even dating back to a time when rulers were buried in the desert sand – clearly stating, 'Cast the sand from your face' in one instance. Another, obviously dating to the time of the great mud-brick mastabas,

c. 1,700–1,550 BC
The Second Intermediate Period. Dynasties XIV–XVII.
The Hyksos invade and conquer much of Egypt.
Only Thebes retains some independence.

This figurine from the troubled First Intermediate period shows an emaciated figure in the midst of famine.

The Great Pyramid

assures the king, 'The bricks are removed for you from the great tomb'. These texts give us vital clues about earlier beliefs.

DECLINE AND FALL

The great age of pyramid building, Dynasties II–VI, is known as the Old Kingdom. At the end of the Old Kingdom, Egypt suffered a troubled time called the First Intermediate Period. There were civil wars, famine and general lawlessness. Offerings in all the Mortuary Temples stopped. The authority of the kings broke down and tombs robbers were out in abundance. Even the Giza pyramids were broken into.

In the First Intermediate Period, few kings lived long enough to build a tomb, but some managed a small pyramid. Meanwhile the Giza giants stood there, reminding people of what had been achieved in the days when Egypt was a prosperous, united country.

NEW PYRAMIDS AND ANCIENT TOURISTS

Most Middle Kingdom pyramids were made of mud bricks with

In the Pyramid Age, coffins and sarcophagi were rectangular in shape. By the New Kingdom, a new style prevailed and people were buried in anthropoid coffins.

only a casing of stone. Once the casing was gone, the wind and sand slowly destroyed the bricks, leaving odd shapes. Sadly, the Middle Kingdom suffered the fate of the Old and collapsed. Egypt's Second Intermediate Period was even worse then the First. The northern part of Egypt was invaded and for over a hundred years was ruled by people from the East, who we know as Hyksos.

The prosperous New Kingdom period began when the Princes of Thebes drove the Hyksos out. As a consequence, Thebes was made the new capital of Egypt. Just before the beginning of the New Kingdom, kings were buried on the West Bank of the Nile at Luxor in tombs described by the Egyptians as pyramids, but this soon changed to tombs cut into the floor and cliff faces of a remote valley that we know as the Valley of the Kings. Interestingly, the mountain that towers over the Valley is shaped exactly like a pyramid. Thebes is too far south to be a convenient site for the capital of a long, narrow country like Egypt. In the New Kingdom, Thebes remained the greatest of

Time line

c. 1,550–1,070 BC

The New Kingdom. Dynasties XVIII–XX.
A Theban prince drives out the Hyksos and reunites Egypt once more. Egypt's great imperial age, when it conquered the greatest empire of its day. Kings are buried in rock-cut tombs in the Valley of Kings at Thebes. The capital is at Thebes, then Memphis.

c. 1,070–664 BC

The Third Intermediate Period. Dynasties XXI–XXV.
Rival Dynasties struggle to control Egypt, with most power in the north. Dynasty XXV rulers come from Nubia, where they are buried in steep-sided pyramids.
The Assyrians invade.

The sphinx towers above the temple built in its honour. It contains the stela that tells the story of the Sphinx and Prince Tuthmosis.

of the great Sphinx at Giza. The Sphinx appeared to him in a dream and said if the prince would have the sand – which had buried the Sphinx up to its neck – cleared away, he would make the prince King of Egypt. The prince did as requested. All his elder brothers died and he became King Tuthmosis IV. He set up a big stela in a little chapel between the paws of the Sphinx, recounting the story of his dream. Besides the problem with the sand, the body of the Sphinx was crumbling in places and work was done to repair it. It was the first of a series of repairs, which took place in the Late Period, under the Greeks and Romans and again in the 20th century. Eventually, the New Kingdom declined, Egypt lost its empire and entered the Third

their holy cities, the centre of the worship of Amun, King of the Gods, and the burial place of kings, queens, other members of the royal family and nobles. Royalty visited the site for festivals and funerals but the government was run from Memphis which meant that the court was once more in the shadow (almost literally) of the Giza pyramids. By this time, Giza and other Old Kingdom pyramids were more than 1,000 years old

and a popular tourist destination. One day-tripper was a scribe who scribbled on a wall that he had visited a pyramid and found it so beautiful – 'as though heaven were within it and the sun rising in it'.

THE SPHINX'S PROMISE

According to legend, one day a prince fell asleep in the shadow

The Great Pyramid was a constant reminder to later generations of Khufu's glory. Perhaps it inspired later kings to build huge monuments of their own.

664–332 BC

The Late Period. Dynasty XXVI–XXX. A native Egyptian dynasty rules and breaks away from the Assyrian Empire, renewing Egypt's greatness. Their capital is Sais. Egypt is twice invaded and becomes part of the Persian Empire, though native rulers constantly try, sometimes successfully, to assert their independence.

The Great Pyramid

These steep-sided pyramids at Meroe in modern-day Sudan are, like so many others, directly influenced by the pyramids at Giza.

Intermediate Period, when a small temple was built against the pyramid of one of Khufu's Queens. It was dedicated to the goddess Isis. Meanwhile the pyramid tradition had found its way south, to the Egyptian province of Nubia. Nubia gained its independence and had its own kings. They and their successors, the kings of the great Kingdom of Meroe, were buried in steep sided stone pyramids at Nuri, el Kurru and Meroe itself, which is in the modern Sudan.

Egyptian greatness was re-established in the Late Period. The Egyptians began studying their ancient history and copied Old Kingdom art styles. They also revived old cults, including those of Khufu, Khafre and Menkawre.

WONDER OF THE WORLD

Late Period kings started hiring Greek soldiers to fight for them and Greek merchants soon flocked to Egypt. Later, Greek and Roman tourists came, fascinated

Time line

332–30 BC
The Ptolemic Period. Egypt is conquered by Alexander the Great. After his death, his general Ptolemy becomes Egypt's king. Alexandria is built and is the capital. The last Ptolemy, the great Cleopatra VII, is defeated by the Romans.

30 BC–AD 641
Egypt is part of the Roman and Byzantine (from AD 395) Empires, during which Egypt becomes Christian.

AD 641–present
The Islamic Period.

by the history and 'strangeness' of the ancient Egyptian culture. Some well-travelled Greeks compiled a list of the most spectacular things they had seen in countries around the Mediterranean – the Seven Wonders of the World. The Giza pyramids are on the list. They were by far the oldest, but they are the only ones to have survived, more or less intact, to the present day. In 332 BC, Alexander the Great conquered Egypt. The family of his General, Ptolemy, then ruled there for some 300 years, until they were overthrown by the Romans. Egypt stayed under the rule of the Romans and their successors in the Middle East, the Byzantines, until the arrival of Muslim invaders in AD 641.

Blocks from the pyramids were used to build Cairo's defences. This shows part of the magnificent walls that guard the Citadel in Cairo. It is built on an outcrop of rock overlooking the city.

A STONE QUARRY

The new rulers were fascinated by the Giza pyramids, especially by the thought that they contained treasure. In the 9th century, the Muslim ruler Ma'mun ordered his men to break into the pyramids. However, any treasure that had once been there had been stolen or removed thousands of years previously. In 969 a new line of Muslim rulers called the Fatimids came to power. They decided to build and fortify a new capital for themselves at Cairo. Close at hand were the Giza pyramids with all their finely cut casing blocks. This proved too tempting a building material to the Fatimids. Therefore, the casing blocks of the Great Pyramid can be seen in the walls of Cairo today.

Alexander, called 'the Great', King of Macedon. When he conquered Egypt, Alexander visited the oasis of Siwa in order to consult the oracle of the god Amun. It is believed the oracle confirmed that Alexander was actually the son of the god Amun.

CHAPTER 3 Explore the pyramids

azing up at the mammoth kings' pyramids at Giza is truly awe-inspiring, and there is even more to see inside. Attached to each pyramid is a complex of temples and buildings that were intended to be the blueprint for the pyramid complexes of Khufu's heirs and successors for hundreds of years. In addition, archaeology is now revealing evidence of how the men who did the actual building were cared for.

Pages 20–21: Inside the Great Pyramid

 1 SUBTERRANEAN CHAMBER

2 QUEEN'S CHAMBER

3 'AIR VENTS'

4 GRAND GALLERY

 5 KING'S CHAMBER

Boat museum

5

4

3

2

1

9

13

11

Sphinx

6

12

The Great Pyramid

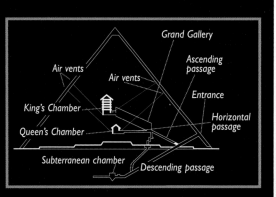

Grand Gallery

Ascending passage

Air vents

Air vents

Entrance

King's Chamber

Horizontal passage

Queen's Chamber

Subterranean chamber

Descending passage

This 19th century engraving shows the entrance to the Horizontal Passage, with the Grand Gallery above it.

1 SUBTERRANEAN CHAMBER

The internal design of the Great Pyramid differs from all other pyramids. It was once thought that it had three chambers because the plans changed during construction, but it is now thought that they were all intended from the start. The lowest room, the SUBTERRANEAN CHAMBER, was cut into the solid rock of the plateau and is reached by the Descending Passage. We are not sure what this chamber was for, but it may have been something to do with the king's passage to the Next World and his well-being there.

2 QUEEN'S CHAMBER

The ASCENDING PASSAGE is very small and you have to bend double to get up through it. It leads to the Horizontal Passage and on to the QUEEN'S CHAMBER. Despite its name, this room was never intended for the burial of a queen. It was probably where a statue of the king was placed.

The passages in the Great Pyramid are often very narrow, such as the Ascending Passage which leads to both the Horizontal Passage and the Grand Gallery.

3 'AIR VENTS'

Leading out of the King's and Queen's Chambers are two passages, just eight inches square, dubbed 'AIR VENTS', one in the north wall and one in the south. None reach the outside of the pyramid and they have nothing to do with bringing air into the pyramid. They are thought to be symbolic passages by which the royal spirit could travel to the stars. A tiny robot has explored the air vents in the Queen's Chamber and found doors at the end – the gates to heaven.

A robot designed specifically to investigate the curious air-vents in the Great Pyramid is sent through those leading out of the Queen's Chamber.

4 GRAND GALLERY

The King's Chamber still contains the bottom half of Khufu's sarcophagus.

Also opening off the Ascending Passage is the magnificent GRAND GALLERY. At the top is the Antechamber, where they stored three slabs of granite. After the burial these were slid into place, sealing off the burial chamber beyond.

Passing through the Grand Gallery involves a very steep climb up to the King's Chamber.

5 KING'S CHAMBER

The KING'S CHAMBER measures approximately 10 x 5 x 5 metres and is built from great granite blocks from Aswan. Nine granite slabs span the roof, each 5 metres long and weighing between 25,000 and 40,000 kilogrammes. The King's **sarcophagus** is also of red granite and was placed at the west end of the room.

The Great Pyramid

Although Khufu's Valley Temple has been destroyed, the massive rose granite pillars of Khafre's temple still stand.

6 VALLEY TEMPLE

The architects placed the **VALLEY TEMPLE** at the point where the desert met the fertile farming land watered by the Nile. It is thought that the King's body may have been mummified here. Khufu's Valley Temple has long since disappeared, but that of his son, Khafre, who built the second pyramid at Giza, has survived. The ground floor of Khafre's Valley Temple contains chambers and a spectacular columned hall. The floor is made of alabaster and the columns are huge blocks of granite. In the late 1980s AD, the Egyptian government funded a new sewage system for the modern town that stands at the foot of the Giza Plateau. When the labourers started digging trenches, however, they found a pavement of black basalt stone – all that is left of Khufu's Valley Temple.

7 CAUSEWAY

Leading up to the Valley Temple of any pyramid was the Causeway – a long covered processional road, decorated with beautifully carved reliefs. Khufu's **CAUSEWAY** has been demolished over the centuries, but traces of it were found at the same time as the pavement of his Valley Temple. Only a few shattered pieces of the reliefs have been found, re-used by a later king in his pyramid.

Although the Great Pyramid's Causeway has been destroyed, we can gain a sense of its grandeur from Pharaoh Unas' Causeway at Sakkara.

8 MORTUARY TEMPLE

The **MORTUARY TEMPLE** was built close to the east side of the pyramid. Some of the funerary rites were probably celebrated there and then offerings would have been made there by the priests every day for ever – or that was the theory anyway. It has been suggested that, at least in later pyramids, this temple may also be seen as a symbolic palace for the king to use in the Afterlife. Khufu's Mortuary Temple has been destroyed, but enough remains to show that it was an impressive building.

Beside the Sphinx is Khafre's Valley Temple. It has two doors. This is the one used by tourists.

9 QUEENS' PYRAMIDS

Recent excavations have revealed that, outside the south-east corner of Khufu's pyramid was a smaller one, only 20 metres long on each side. This pyramid is believed to have been for the King's 'ka' – or part of his soul. To the east of this pyramid are three larger pyramids that were built for Khufu's queens. Each has a passage leading down to an antechamber and a burial chamber. Close by, at the bottom of a deep shaft were found the remains of the burial of Khufu's mother, Hetep-heres.

This well-preserved chair from Hetep-heres' tomb is one of many beautiful items excavated at Giza.

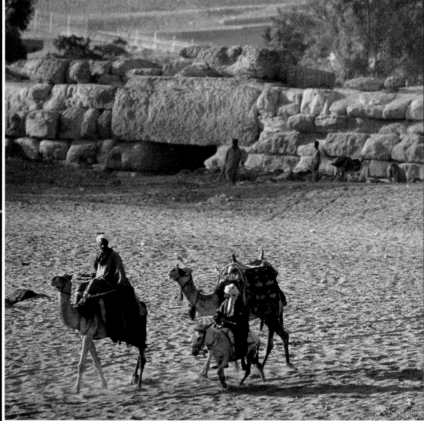

The massive wall now called the Wall of the Crow divided the workmen's village from the sacred site at Giza.

▲10 BARRACKS FOR UNSKILLED LABOURERS

The unskilled labourers who worked on the pyramids lived in barracks on the western edge of the site at Giza. These contained kitchens and canteens, and workshops for the craftsmen. In order to get the stone from distant quarries, and all the other supplies that were needed, as close to the building site as possible (so reducing the distance they had to be dragged overland to a minimum), a huge harbour was excavated at the foot of the plateau. Hundreds of men were needed to dig out the massive harbour, which was then lined with stone. The water was supplied by a canal connected to the Nile. This in itself was an amazing feat of engineering.

▲11 ANCIENT SITE OF KHUFU'S PALACE

Khufu needed a palace nearby, where he could stay when he came to visit the site and inspect the progress of the work. It may not have been as large as the one at Memphis, but it still had to be fit for the god-king, his family, chief courtiers and servants. It was built to the east of the pyramid, with the Valley Temple to the north and the harbour to the south. Giza must have been one of the noisiest, most dusty sites in the whole of Egypt. Some of this must have penetrated into the cool comfort of the palace.

This is a view from the top of Khufu's pyramid. The remains of what may have been Khufu's palace are visible nearby.

▲12 OLD KHUFU SETTLEMENT

The craftsmen had to have proper houses for themselves and their families. Even after the king's burial, craftsmen would still be needed to provide new ritual vessels for the priests and to see to repairs. The priests, their families and their descendents, who would make offerings to Khufu's spirit for ever, expected to be given large, comfortable houses near their work. The architects therefore built 'Gerget Khufu', the Settlement of Khufu, pleasantly situated on the south side of the harbour with rolling fields beyond its eastern boundary. Like Khufu's Valley Temple, the remains of the town, the palace and the harbour were located during the great sewer installation project of the 1980s and 90s.

In the late 20th century, the remains of Giza's old settlement were excavated. This is where the pyramids' many craftsmen and their families were housed.

▲13 NOBLES' MASTABAS

Impressive tombs also had to built for the other members of the royal family and the most important courtiers. These tombs were large stone mastabas. The rooms were decorated with top quality relief carvings which were painted in bright colours. The mastabas were arranged in neat rows, like houses along streets. The more important you were, the nearer your mastaba was to the king's pyramid, so Khufu would have the services of his family and courtiers in the Next World, as in this one.

Noblemen and other people of importance were buried in elaborate tombs called 'mastabas'.

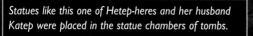

Statues like this one of Hetep-heres and her husband Katep were placed in the statue chambers of tombs.

CHAPTER 4

The people

Ｗe know very little about the personalities and private lives of the royal family of Dynasty IV, because so few written documents survived. Also, the Egyptians believed that, if you wrote something down, it would go on happening. So, they were careful not to record things like rebellions or family feuds among the royal family. We do, however, know a little about some of the royal family, the Egyptian gods and the people who helped build the pyramids from the artifacts they left behind.

THE ROYAL FAMILY

Khufu is thought to have had three queens, hence the three pyramids beside his at Giza. The chief queen was his sister-wife Meritites, who was the mother of Crown Prince Kawab and Hetep-heres II. Kawab died before his father and Redjedef, son of Khufu by another queen became king.

This gilded chest filled with silver bracelets decorated with jewel-encrusted butterflies was discovered in Queen Hetep-heres' tomb at Giza.

He reigned only a short time and was succeeded by Khafre, the son of the third queen of Khufu. Khafre had at least two queens. One was his niece, Meresankh III, daughter of Kawab and Hetep-heres II. The other queen bore Khafre's heir, Menkawre.

Based on evidence gleaned from their mastaba tombs, some scholars believe there was a power struggle for the throne between Redjedef and Khafre and that the feud persisted between their children. If there was such a feud, it was healed when Userkaf, first king of Dynasty V thought to be descended from Redjedef, married Khentkawes, daughter of Menkawre.

EARTHLY GODS

Kings were considered so holy, so full of magic power, that even to touch one by mistake could kill a person. The gods gave the king the authority, the power and the wisdom to rule well. It was believed that he could even control the Inundation, ensuring a good annual flood

Tale & customs – A CLEVER TRICK

When men plotted against the sun god Re, he sent the goddess Hathor to punish them. She transformed herself into a fierce lioness called Sekhmet and set about killing all of mankind. Alarmed by this turn of events, Re had 7,000 jars of beer dyed red to look like blood and flooded the fields with it. Sekhmet, thinking it was blood, lapped it up, became very drunk and happy and turned back into the lovely, gentle Hathor. So mankind was saved.

watered the fields. The king simply could not fail – in theory anyway. To enforce his policies and carry out the day-to-day business of government, the king used hundreds of officials. All the top posts in government in Dynasty IV were held by the kings' relatives – uncles, brothers, cousins – but they in their turn had their staff to advise them and to do the actual work.

THE PLANNERS

The most important official, the head of all branches of the government, was the

The seated scribe above holds a papyrus roll stretched across his knees. His well-fed appearance gives an impression of success in life.

This statue of Khafre, who built the second pyramid at Giza, shows him with a falcon with its wings around his head. The falcon symbolises Khafre's relationship with the god Horus.

vizier. The vizier had total responsibility for the pyramid project. His job was to co-ordinate the efforts of the craftsmen and make sure everything ran smoothly. The chief architect and his assistants were in charge of planning and building. They had to be experts in architecture, engineering, mathematics and geometry. In addition to the pyramid complex itself the

The Great Pyramid

One of the many tasks involved in building the pyramids was making mud-bricks, as is shown in this detail from a New Kingdom wall painting. This painting is from the tomb of the vizier Rekhmira at the Valley of the Nobles at Qurna.

architects had to provide the living quarters for the workmen, and for the priests who would serve in the Mortuary Temple. The workers also excavated a huge artificial harbour and a canal that connected it to the Nile. This meant that boats carrying stone blocks could sail right up close to the site, cutting down the distance the blocks needed to be dragged over land.

KEEPING TRACK OF THINGS

Alongside the architects were the officials and their staff of scribes. Their task was to acquire, and organise the arrival of, all the different supplies needed to keep the project running. The officials had to organise the thousands of workers. A fleet of ships had to be built to transport the great number of workers from all over Egypt to the pyramid site at Giza. Once on

site, the thousands of men had to be housed, fed and kept in good health. A steady supply of food had to come from the royal storehouses and an army of cooks, bakers and brewers had to be assembled. Another vital task for officials was to arrange the transport of the stone blocks by river from their various quarries. Timing was crucial. The Nile flooded every year between mid-

June and mid-October. Its waters spread across the land, right up to the desert edge. The aim was to have as many blocks as possible ready for transport when the waters started rising. In addition to men, food and stone, supplies of wood, metal and ropes were also needed for the workmen's tools and equipment.

These tools from the tomb of a New Kingdom architect give archaeologists an idea of how ancient Egyptian building was carried out.

Tale & customs – A HUNGRY SERPENT

The ancient Egyptians believed that when the sun god Re sailed through the Underworld at night, he would encounter a monstrous serpent called Apophis, who would try to swallow him. Sometimes the god Set defeated Apophis for Re. Other times, the Great Cat of Re would pounce on the snake, and chop it into pieces with a knife. However the serpent was defeated each night, as long as Re survived, he would be be born again the next morning in the east.

THE SKILLED WORKFORCE

Foremost among the craftsmen were the masons. Unskilled men could cut blocks from quarries, but experts had to choose the right stone and show the labourers how to prise blocks from the quarry. Skilled workers, however, were needed to shape and finish each block.

Egypt's best sculptors were also needed. The inside walls of the Causeway were covered with fine relief sculptures and there would have been dozens of statues of Khufu in both the Mortuary and the Valley Temples. All tools, sledges and ropes constantly needed repairing or replacing, so many carpenters, metalsmiths and ropemakers were employed on site too. Archaeologists have found the remains of the workshops where some of the craftsmen worked at Giza.

OTHER WORKERS

Although they did not work on the actual building site, boat-builders were of vital importance to the pyramid-building project. Large wooden boats were required for

Boatbuilders, as illustrated in this temple painting from Sakkara, were among the thousands of workers required at Giza. The River Nile was the most effective route for delivering equipment and supplies.

carrying the heavy blocks of stone from quarry to site.

As native Egyptian trees did not make good-quality timber, it had to be imported. Their best source was the country now called Lebanon, which had forests of magnificent cedar trees. People working on the pyramid sometimes fell ill and, of course, there were accidents resulting in broken bones or crushed limbs.

The Great Pyramid

The king assumed responsibility for their welfare and employed doctors to look after them on site.

UNSKILLED WORKFORCE

In the days before money was invented, people used a system called barter (an exchange of goods and services). Similarly, taxes had to be paid in goods and services. Farmers gave part of their crops as taxes to the king and craftsmen gave some of the things they made. It is also generally assumed that people had to pay the king a tax in the form of work – in a mine or quarry on a royal building project.

Of course, not everyone would have been called up for service at once. Across the country, probably only one in 100 were called up at any given time, so, once you had done a stint, it would be a long time before your services would be required again. Officials travelled around the country with lists of men who were due to do their work tax. The men were shipped to Giza, where they served for only three months at a time. They were fed, housed,

This figurine shows a potter at work. Potters would have been amongst the many craftsmen at Giza.

clothed and provided with oil (to keep their skin clean and supple) by the king.

COMPULSORY EFFORT

The best time for a man who owned a farm to do his work tax was when the Nile flood had covered his fields, but to get the pyramid completed there needed to be unskilled workers labouring throughout the year also, so arrangements would have to be made for others to do their work outside the flood season.

It is estimated that there would usually be about 20,000 unskilled labourers on site at one time. Recent excavations at Giza have shown that the men were well fed. Besides bread and beer, the basic items in any ancient Egyptian meal, the workmen also enjoyed a wide variety of meat, fish, vegetables and fruit. Each 'gang' of 10 people probably bunked together in the barracks.

THE GIZA GANGS

Each gang had a name and some were not at all respectful. For instance, one gang working on the third Giza pyramid, that of King Menkawre, called themselves 'The Drunkards of Menkawre'. There may even have been some rivalry between gangs to see who could shift the most blocks, inspiring them to take names like 'The Enduring Gang'. These men believed that by

This photograph illustrates the kind of bread-making on an industrial scale that would have taken place at Giza for the thousands of pyramid workers.

working to guarantee the journey of their god-king to the Afterlife, they were ensuring their own future in the Next World. They had served him, and therefore, he would see that they were well treated after death – as he had cared for them while they worked

This wall painting shows the sheer numbers required to transport a colossal statue.

on his pyramid. At the end of their three-month stint, the men would be shipped home and a new batch would arrive, but it is possible that, if a man was a landless labourer at home, he might choose to train and become one of the permanent labour force.

Tale & customs – YOU SILLY GOOSE!

One Egyptian legend, circulating by the time of the Middle Kingdom period, tells of the great priest-magician Dedi. When Dedi was the grand old age of 110 years old, Khufu summoned him to Court to demonstrate his powers. At the King's command, a goose was brought in and its head was cut off. Dedi recited various prayers and spells which resulted in the head and body of the goose moving back together and joining up once more. The goose then ran off cackling.

CHAPTER 5

A day in the life

The Giza Plateau is one of the most popular destinations for the modern tourist. With its towering pyramids – or, the 'Mountains of Pharaoh', as early Arab writers called them – Giza attracts two million tourists every year. Daytime attractions include exploring inside the pyramids, camel rides and shopping. Evening entertainment includes the 'Sound and Light' show and, occasionally, an open-air production of Verdi's opera Aida.

JOURNEY IN COMFORT

The journey between Cairo and Giza used to be through open fields. Indeed, when the Empress Eugenie of France went to Egypt for the opening of the Suez Canal in 1869, the Khedive Ishmael had to build a road through farmland, just so she could visit the pyramids comfortably in her carriage.

However, in the late 20th century, Cairo started growing rapidly and now its suburbs sprawl right up to the foot of the desert cliff on which the pyramids are built. With the hundreds of flats, hotels and villas came spectacular traffic jams and long delays on the drive between the centre of Cairo and Giza. Now, however, a new motorway system has made the journey much quicker and easier.

FOLLOW THE CROWD

The day starts early at Giza. By 8 o'clock hoards of tourists are

Today, luxury hotels have been built right up to the foot of the Giza Plateau.

arriving via coaches, mini-buses and taxis. More and more visitors arrive during the day and when a cruise liner docks in Alexandria, hundreds of passengers are driven on an exhausting – though exhilarating – day trip that takes in the magnificent sites at Cairo and Giza. The plateau is even more crowded than usual at those times. Besides the tourists there are usually also several groups of excited Egyptian school children, studying the history of their country at first hand.

In order to reduce the damage inside the Great Pyramid, the number of tourists allowed in is now restricted (see p. 44). Twice a day, only a limited number of tickets is sold. It is not advisable to go through the Great Pyramid if you have breathing problems, a bad back or stiff knees. In some passages you have to scramble through bent double, while the Grand Gallery is a very steep climb.

One of many daily groups of tourists gathers around their Guide to hear about the Sphinx and Khafre's Valley Temple.

The pyramids at Giza are guarded by the tourist police guard. The most impressive-looking security division is the Camel Corps, shown here attending an annual festival.

TOURISTS BEWARE

Once out of their coaches, tourists are pounced on by salesmen, who offer everything the tourist could want – postcards, stamps, sunhats, guide books, cool drinks, Bedouin headscarves, model pyramids, toy camels and imitation ancient

Tale & customs – KHUFU'S ROYAL LINE

An Egyptian legend states that, when questioned about the future by Khufu, the priest-magician Dedi told the King that only his son and grandson would reign after him. In fact, the main male line did die out with Khufu's grandson. However, the next (Fifth) dynasty of kings were descended from a granddaughter and a great-granddaughter of Khufu. Dedi's prophecies about the kings of the Fifth Dynasty are written in the 'Westcar Papyrus'. Re is said to have aided these kings in their rise to power.

*Verdi's opera **Aida** (which is set in Egypt) is often performed in an open-air theatre before the grand backdrop of the pyramids.*

Egyptian jewellery figurines. Besides the salesmen there are men with camels, horses and donkeys for hire.

ROUND AND ABOUT

After exploring the Great Pyramid, visitors often drive around the back of the pyramids to a desert ridge that has become known as 'Viewpoint'. Because of their great size, it is very difficult to photograph all three pyramids together, but at Viewpoint it is possible. If visitors do not go inside the Great Pyramid, they may choose to go inside those of Khafre or Menkawre.

A visit to the boat museum, which houses the funeral boat of Khufu, is an extraordinary sight.

Many tourists accept the offer of a ride on a 'ship of the desert' and make sure someone takes a photo of them, so they can prove they did it.

34

Tale & customs – LORD OF THE BOAT

Coptic legend tells of a king who built the Giza pyramids and filled them with treasure, statues and scrolls full of scientific knowledge. He did this because he had dreamed that one day there would be a catastrophic inundation or flood that would destroy everything. Only those who joined the 'Lord of the Boat' would survive. No-one knows who the Lord of the Boat was believed to be, but it is clear that he is a combination of the biblical Noah and the Egyptian god Re.

As you enter the museum you have to put on canvas slippers over your shoes. This is to protect the wooden floor from being damaged by people's shoes. Staircases and galleries wind all around the boat.

In winter, when it is often quite cloudy, tourists might linger into the late afternoon. If they are lucky, sun rays sometimes shine through the clouds, outlining one or other of the pyramids with an aura of light, recalling the spell in the *Pyramid Texts*, which promises the king a ramp of sunbeams, upon which he can walk to heaven.

NIGHT-TIME ENTERTAINMENT

As the daytime tourists leave, the Giza Plateau prepares itself for a new influx of people. Every evening there are 'Sound and Light' shows at the pyramids – usually two performances a night and in different languages, thus catering for tourists from all over the world, as well as local Cairo residents.

Behind the pyramids there is an open-air theatre. This is where they sometimes have performances of Verdi's great romantic opera, set in ancient Egypt, *Aida*. It was actually written to celebrate the opening of the Suez Canal. There is no more dramatic backdrop for *Aida* than the pyramids themselves.

The Sphinx glowing in the unearthly lights of a 'Sound and Light' performance at Giza.

CHAPTER 6

Significant events

A newly discovered inscription shows that Khufu reigned at least 27 years, not 24 as was previously thought. Even so, his pyramid was not quite finished when he died. The Subterranean Chamber, for example, was not ready, but work stopped. The funeral, which was the whole purpose of the pyramid, had to take place and then the eternal cycle of offerings to the King's spirit began.

DEATH BY THE NILE

No records exist that explain how a king's body was prepared for burial. However, we know about the process for wealthy commoners. The king's would have been essentially the same – just on a grander scale.

When Khufu died, the whole palace would have been plunged into very noisy mourning – with people wailing, tearing their hair and throwing dirt over their heads. The embalmers would then arrive, accompanied by a priest called a 'lector priest', who would have recited prayers and rituals, and two priestesses known as the 'kites'. They would then have taken the body, perhaps on one of the boats discovered at Giza (see pp. 40–41), down-stream to the pyramid site.

The mummy of Nefer from the tomb of Nefer and Waty at Sakkara is so well-preserved that the facial features are quite clearly intact even after thousands of years.

MUMMIFICATION

Khufu's body would then be taken to a building called the 'ibu'. There the body purification and prayers would have taken place, and the embalming process begun. The brain and the internal organs would then be removed and taken away to be preserved separately. Once these messy stages of the process were completed, the ibu could then be swept away without trace. The body would then be moved to the wabet ('Pure Place'), a mud-brick building also near the river. The wabet used for Khufu would not be the one used by his subjects. His was attached to his Valley Temple, perhaps on the flat roof. There his body would have been covered with a special salt called natron, which would draw out all the water. It would then be wrapped up in linen bandages. The whole process took 70 days and was accompanied by prayers, rituals and magic spells.

Tale & customs – THE BIRD AND THE BOOTY

An Arab legend describes the first raid on the Great Pyramid as occurring in AD 820. According to the legend, when Caliph al-Mamun's men broke into Khufu's pyramid, they were greeted by a golden cockerel, inlaid with precious stones, that actually flapped its wings and crowed! There was also a body, covered in rubies, in a gold box and a water jar that never ran dry. However, according to the highly respected Arab historian Abu Szalt who went in with Mamun's men, all they really found were a few bones.

This Old Kingdom relief from Sakkara shows people bearing offerings to the king's tomb.

amid clouds of incense, a special ceremony called 'Opening of the Mouth' gave the dead king the power to speak, hear, smell, eat, breath and move. He had become an 'effective' spirit.

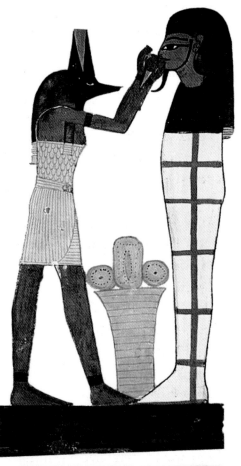

This New Kingdom painting shows a priest performing the 'Opening of the Mouth' ceremony on a mummy.

THE FUNERAL

Finally, the body in its wooden coffin would have been carried to the tomb, accompanied by an éntourage, along with an army of servants carrying offerings – food of all kinds, wine, beer, furniture, clothes, perfumes and cosmetics, tools and weapons, jewellery and treasure – every conceivable thing that the king would need to enjoy the Next World. At some point, perhaps in the Mortuary Temple,

CHAPTER 7

Uncovering the past

When Christianity became the official religion of the Roman Empire, ancient Egyptian hieroglyphs were no longer used. Ancient knowledge, ideas and customs were forgotten. Strange stories grew up around the Giza pyramids: they were built to escape Noah's flood, or they were the granaries built by Joseph to store grain in the seven years of plenty, or they were a store to protect books of secret wisdom.

EUROPEANS DISCOVER EGYPT

Because of the bad relations between Christians and Muslims during the Crusades of the Middle Ages (fought between 1095 and 1291), very few Europeans visited Egypt for centuries afterwards. Still, a few did make it, at least to Giza, between the 16th and 18th centuries. They published accounts of their adventures but, in the days before cameras, the illustrations were rarely accurate. Everything changed after 1798 when Napoleon Bonaparte invaded Egypt. Napoleon was impressed by the Giza pyramids. Just before a crucial battle, it is said that he pointed to the pyramids and shouted, 'Soldiers! Forty centuries look down upon you from these pyramids'. Attached to his army he had a group of scholars, whose task was to travel throughout Egypt, producing accurate descriptions and drawings of all its ancient monuments. The publication of their great *Description de l'Egypte*, combined with Champollion's discovery of how to read ancient hieroglyphs, caught people's imagination. This started a fascination with ancient Egyptian history, which continues to this day.

Jean-Francois Champollion's ideas on how to read hieroglyphs were published in 1822.

In the 19th century scholars swarmed over Egypt, exploring its great monuments – such as at Abu Simbel (pictured).

RUTHLESS COLLECTORS

In the 19th century, people went to Egypt to explore the monuments and to bring back souvenirs, for museums or their own private collections. People were fascinated by beautiful, magnificent (and valuable) works of art, such as statues, reliefs, paintings and jewellery. Some even thought it was impressive to own an ancient mummy. A great deal of damage and robbery resulted. One man even blasted his way into Khafre's pyramid with dynamite.

CURIOUS THEORIES

People have always been fascinated by the pyramids, especially the Giza group and Khufu's Great Pyramid, in particular. Nineteenth century archaeologists analysed it – measuring, drawing and recording. But there were those who found it difficult to believe that the Great Pyramid was 'just' a tomb. One such enthusiast was Charles Piazzi Smyth. Having measured every bit of the pyramid he decided that the whole thing was based on a measurement he called the 'pyramid inch'. He believed that the measurements of the pyramid, its chambers and passages, were the result of a set of prophecies, inspired by God, foretelling events in the history of the world, besides confirming certain events in the Bible and revealing such scientific details as the circumference of the Earth. He and his followers have been dubbed 'pyramidiots' by scholars.

In the 19th century, many theories arose about the Great Pyramid having mystical origins. In this illustration, Egyptian priests survey the stars from a chamber within the Great Pyramid.

Tale & customs – IN HIS FATHER'S IMAGE

Hordedef was one of Khufu's sons. Hordedef was himself revered as a wise man, but only a fragment of his teachings have survived. In them, he gives his readers practical advice on how to behave and recommends that they prepare for the future, both in this world and the next. Legend says he discovered some secret books of wisdom. These are said to have been incorporated into the Book of the Dead, an important text that was used in burials during the New Kingdom.

The Great Pyramid

Tale & customs – A TALKING SPHINX?

The Sphinx fascinated the early European explorers. The German Johannes Helferich, who was in Egypt in the later 16th century, claimed that there was a secret passage in the Sphinx, where priests would hide and fool the people into believing the Sphinx was speaking to them. The fact that, in his book, Helferich illustrated the Sphinx as female (representing the goddess Isis) does not do much for his credibility. No passages or chambers have been detected in the Sphinx to date.

ALL THE KING'S BOATS

Five boat-shaped graves around the Great Pyramid have been known about for hundreds of years. Then, in 1954, two more pits were discovered. Both were roofed over by huge limestone slabs. When the roof was removed from the first pit, the dismantled remains of a large wooden boat were revealed. As archaeologists removed the boat, piece by piece, they realised that, thanks to Egypt's dry climate, the wood was in such miraculously good condition that it might be possible to rebuild the 4,500 year old boat. It was made of cedar wood and the planks were originally lashed together with ropes. There were 1,224 separate parts to reassemble and it took many years.

The earliest Nile boats were made of bundles of papyrus reeds. Though made of cedar wood, the prow and stern of Khufu's boat are carved to represent the bound bundles of reeds of earlier times.

Only a few pieces were too warped or decayed to use, and so those were replaced by modern replicas. Modern rope had to be used, although they did find a great coil of the original rope. The boat now rests in its own museum, which also covers the pit where it was found. The boat is 43 metres long, a vessel of elegance and breathtaking beauty.

In 1985 a tiny camera was lowered through a hole drilled in one of the roof blocks of the second pit. It too contained a dismantled boat, which has been left in its pit. Burying boats was not actually a new idea. The remains of boats, or the graves that once contained them, have been found in royal graves dating back to Dynasty I. However, it was certainly unusual for Khufu to have seven.

SAILING INTO ETERNITY

It seems likely that the seven Khufu boats were intended for different purposes. The reconstructed boat may be the

A Middle Kingdom model of a Nile boat. Note the square sail and large steering oar.

actual vessel that carried Khufu's dead body to his pyramid. If so, that would have made it a very holy object, that could not be used

One of the empty boat graves at Giza.

again. Perhaps by taking it apart and burying it, they thought its power would be safely contained. Other boats may have been used

by the royal family in life and had been sent to join them in the Next World, so that they could go on using them there.

SAILING WITH RE

The Egyptians imagined that Re travelled by boat along a heavenly Nile, on his journey across the sky. When he was reborn in the east each day he boarded one boat to use on his journey to the west. In the evening he boarded another boat, which was to take him through the Underworld, bringing light to the realm governed by Osiris, god of the dead, and his subjects. Perhaps the Egyptians thought the king would need boats of his own, if he was to travel with Re across the heavens of the realms of the living and the dead and clearly Khufu was not a king who did things by halves – especially where his own glory and comfort in the Next World were concerned.

CAT scans are a way for archaeologists to examine mummies without having to unwrap their bandages and potentially damage the fragile remains.

ARCHAEOLOGY AND SCIENCE

In the late 19th century, an archaeologist named Flinders Petrie introduced scientific methods into Egyptian archaeology. Museums and universities mounted expeditions to study sites in depth. George Reisner, Hermann Junker and Selim Hassan excavated many nobles' tombs at Giza and published their findings in great detail.

Most importantly, however, new rules were introduced about digging in Egypt and the removal of artifacts. Any excavator had to get a licence to dig from the Egyptian Antiquities Service and it was recognised that the objects they found belonged to the Egyptian people. Excavators were to receive a share of their finds. But the best pieces, the unique objects, were to stay in Egypt. These basic rules still apply.

Tale & customs – SECRET NAMES

Each Egyptian god and goddess had a secret name, which was the source of his or her magic powers. One day Re was stung by a magic scorpion, put in his path by his cunning great-granddaughter Isis. Re was in agony. Only Isis could cure him. She said she would do so, but only if he told her his secret name. In the end, Re had to give in and she cured him. This meant that she now possessed Re's powers as well as her own, and therefore became the greatest of all magicians.

NEW FINDS AT GIZA

Archaeology has come a long way since 1880, when Petrie first went to Egypt to measure the Giza pyramids. Nowadays, besides looking for precious artifacts, archaeologists are also looking for things that, although worthless in themselves, are incredibly valuable because of what they can tell us about the lives of ordinary Egyptians, like the men who built the Great Pyramid.

In the 1980s, new excavations began at Giza and are still going on today. The centre of interest is now not the pyramids or the nobles' tombs, but the people who built them. To find them, the archaeologists had to look outside the main, sacred areas. They uncovered the workshops, barracks, canteens and kitchens of the thousands who laboured to build the magnificent monuments. The work is being most carefully conducted, so that even tiny

This papyrus from the Book of the Dead shows a deceased person purifying offerings by pouring water over them.

This jewel-encrusted necklace is one of the many treasures excavated from Pharaoh Tutankhamun's tomb.

things like fruit pips and fish bones are recovered, giving valuable information about the workmen's diet.

IN KHUFU'S SHADOW

Archaeologists also recovered the cemetery of the men (usually members of the permanent workforce) and their families, who died during the course of construction. Over a thousand graves have been

discovered so far and, interestingly, some have small mud-brick pyramids built over the top. These remains, which only a few years ago would have received little attention, are now carefully examined. They reveal details about the person's diet, medical history and age at death. The worn backbone of one of these men shows that he had once done hard physical labour, presumably hauling stones for the pyramid. But the inscriptions in his tomb reveal that, when he died, he was an important Overseer. Here is critical evidence that an ordinary Egyptian could rise up through the ranks of society.

CHAPTER 8

Preserving the past

All over the world, people are fascinated by ancient Egypt. Its architecture, furniture and jewellery have been imitated and adapted for modern tastes and it has inspired numerous films, from great Hollywood biblical epics to horror and sci-fi movies.

OUR DUTY TO THE PHARAOHS

Once only the very wealthy could afford to visit Egypt. That changed in 1869, when a Mr Thomas Cook began offering package holidays in Egypt at modest prices. Now thousands of tourists flock to Egypt every year and one of the first things they see is the Great Pyramid and the other monuments of the Giza Plateau.

But tourists can damage the very wonders they have come to admire. Roads have been built across sites and coaches rumble around, causing vibrations that can damage the monuments. Thousands of feet trampling on ancient pavements do them no good and, at Giza, the pollution from the ever-growing city of Cairo is a problem. Just as bad is the effect of humans inside a monument. Their breath and perspiration leaves the air damp, which damages the stones.

Efforts are being made to preserve the monuments throughout Egypt, but it is also up to those lucky enough to visit the ancient sites to obey some simple rules. Don't lean on the walls as the salty sweat from your body will destroy paint and delicate carvings; don't use flash lights as it destroys colours in the paint; and don't carve your name on the walls.

MODERN TECHNOLOGY

Increasing numbers of scientific techniques are now available to archaeologists. These help provide a better understanding of the things discovered – right down to the last fish bone, insect-wing

A modern craftsman uses ancient techniques to carve a block to repair a building. The building may even have been worked on by his remote ancestors.

Tale & customs – AN END TO FAMINE

During the reign of King Zoser, Egypt suffered seven years of famine. Zoser consulted his wise minister, Imhotep, who told him that the god Khnum was responsible for withholding the Nile's annual flood. Zoser prayed to Khnum, who appeared to him in a dream. The two made a deal. Zoser agreed to build Khnum a temple and endow it with land and, in return, Khnum promsied to send good floods and bumper harvests. So ended the seven years of famine.

By keeping the Sphinx uncovered, so it may all be seen, we have made it vulnerable to the abrasive effects of wind-blown sand. Major repair work has recently been done to preserve it.

ancient DNA will help us build up information on the family ties and racial origins of groups of mummies.

EXPERIMENTAL ARCHAEOLOGY

To understand and appreciate the skills of ancient craftsmen and builders, some archaeologists try to make things the way the ancients did. At Giza they even built a small pyramid to see if their theories about building techniques worked in practice. Modern architects sometimes use a pyramid shape for buildings, but in modern materials – concrete, steel and glass. They are often very impressive, of course, but nothing can compare with the real thing. Gazing up at the mountainous Great Pyramid is a thrilling experience. It truly is one of the wonders of the world.

case and seed. Computers can take information supplied by archaeologists about a ruined building and show us how it looked when new. New medical techniques and equipment are invaluable tools in studying and preserving the past. For example, a CAT scan can give us a picture of the body and skeleton of a mummy without removing the bandages and so destroying the specimen. We even have tiny cameras that allow us to look inside the body, without cutting it open. Soon, advances in recovering

The glass pyramid that was built in front of the Louvre Museum, Paris.

45

Glossary

Afterlife Life after death. Also known by the Egyptions as the Next World.

Amun Amun began his rise to power as patron of the kings of Dynasty XII. Later, he was identified with Re and became Amun-Re, King of the Gods. The ram was one of his sacred animals.

Anthropoid Human-shaped.

Anubis God of embalming, guardian of the dead. His sacred animal was a jackal.

Capstone The pointed stone placed at the top of a pyramid.

Casing blocks Finely cut and polished blocks that form the outer layer of a pyramid.

Cataract A place where outcrops of rock interrupt the flow of the Nile. There are six cataracts, the first is at Aswan, the sixth is just North of Khartoum.

Causeway In Egypt it refers to a stone-built, roofed passage that connects the Valley and Mortuary Temples of straight-sided pyramids.

Citadel A fortress built on high ground above a city.

Coptic The branch of the Christian Church that evolved in Egypt. It comes from the Greek word for Egypt.

Dynasty A family of rulers.

Hathor One of Egypt's oldest and most powerful goddesses, a mother who protects her worshippers in this world and the Next. Her sacred animal was a cow.

Horus One of Egypt's most ancient gods, Horus was god of the sky and of kingship. The falcon was his sacred bird.

Ibu A tent where a body was taken in preparation for burial. The 'ibu' was also called 'the place of purification'.

Inundation In Egypt, a land virtually without rain, people depended on the Nile's annual flood. To stress its importance to Egypt, it is commonly referred to as 'the Inundation'.

Isis Great-granddaughter of Re, wife of her brother Osiris and mother of Horus. When her husband was murdered, she helped restore him to life. She was also a mother goddess.

Ka One of the three parts that made up an ancient Egyptian's soul. The ka represents a person's individual personality. It was in human form and needed food and provisions to enjoy the Afterlife.

Khnum God of the First Cataract, controller of the Nile. He fashioned people's bodies and spirits on his potter's wheel.

Khufu, Khafre and Menkawre These are as near as we can get to the ancient names for these kings. In some books you will find them referred to as Cheops, Chephren and Mycerinus – the Greek versions of their names.

Mastaba A rectangular tomb, built of stone or mud brick, on the surface of the desert. The body was usually buried in an underground chamber.

Mortuary Temple The temple built against the side of a pyramid. There the priests were supposed to make daily offerings to the dead king's spirit for all eternity.

Mummification Egyptian method of preserving the body after death by removing the internal organs, embalming it and wrapping it in bandages.

Next World Where the Egyptians believed the human spirit travelled to after death.

Nubia The land to the south of Egypt. It was an important trading partner of Egypt.

Opening of the Mouth A ritual performed during any ancient Egyptian funeral. It gave back to the dead person the power to speak, breath, feel and move.

Oracle Advice or instructions given by a god or goddess, usually through their priests.

Osiris God of the Dead, ruler of the Underworld, he became one of Egypt's most popular deities. He was murdered by his jealous brother, Set, but brought back to life by Isis and Horus, his sister-wife and son. Because he had been resurrected, the ancient Egyptians believed that, through him, they too would be born again and live for ever.

Overseer Title used by every senior- or middle-ranking official in every level of the ancient Egyptian administration.

Pharaoh This comes from two ancient Egyptian words *per-aa*, meaning 'great house'. It was a respectful way of referring to the King. It was not used as a title until the New Kingdom.

Pyramid Texts Spells, hymns and prayers, meant to protect the king and ensure his safe passage to the Next World. They were carved on the walls of the burial chambers of pyramids. They first appear in the pyramid of Unas, the last king of Dynasty V. However, it is clear from the content that they were already hundreds of years old even then.

Re The sun god, one of Egypt's most important deities. His main temple was at Heliopolis, a few miles north of Memphis. His sacred animal was a bull.

Sarcophagus A stone coffin. Only royalty and nobles could afford these expensive items. The body was put in a wooden coffin and then placed in the sarcophagus.

Scribe Official person in ancient Egypt who copied out documents and recorded all the important events in writing.

Sphinx A version of the sun god. The one at Giza is the most famous, but there were many other, smaller ones. They usually have a human (royal) head and the body of a lion.

Stela An upright slab of stone (or sometimes wood) with inscriptions carved or written on it. The inscriptions are usually religious, but some kings set up a stela to record a special event.

The Two Lands Egyptians never forgot that they had started out as two separate kingdoms – Upper (southern) and Lower (northern) Egypt. Upper Egypt stretched from the 1st Cataract to the place where the Nile divides, where modern Cairo now stands. There, the Nile divides into several channels and flows through Lower Egypt to the Mediterranean Sea.

Thoth God of wisdom and medicine. His sacred creatures were the ibis and the baboon. His main temple was at Hermopolis.

Underworld Another realm inhabited by the dead. Similar to the Christian concept of Hell as it was believed to be filled with fiery lakes and volcanoes. Every night the god Re was believed to sail through the Underworld where he had to defeat the angry Sun in order to ensure the Sun rose again on the new day.

Valley Temple A temple in a straight-sided pyramid complex. It stood where the valley met the desert.

Vizier Next-ranking officer to the pharaoh and his closest adviser.

Index

Copyright © ticktock Entertainment Ltd 2005
First published in Great Britain in 2005 by ticktock Media Ltd.,
Unit 2, Orchard Business Centre, North Farm Road, Tunbridge Wells, Kent, TN2 3XF
We would like to thank: Alison Howard, Susan Barraclough, Elizabeth Wiggans and Jenni Rainford for their help with this book.
Printed in China. A CIP catalogue record for this book is available from the British Library.

Picture Credits
Alamy: 32, 33L, 35R; Art Archive: 1, 5L, 6, 9, 11T, 11B, 13L, 14, 15L, 16, 17L, 17R, 18L, 19L, 19R, 20R, 21BR, 22B, 23B, 26, 27L, 27R, 28T, 28–9, 30, 37L, 38, 40, 43T; British Museum: 25BL; Corbis: 2–3, 21T, 21BL, 25BR, 33R, 34T, 34B, 42, 44, 45T; Heritage Images: 23T, 39R; National Geographic: 15R, 18–19, 24T, 24B, 31T, 36, 39T; Werner Forman 5R, 12, 13R, 22TR.